KU-767-644

CONTENTS

SYMBOLS KEY

The following symbols are used throughout this book:

ⓐ address **ⓣ** telephone **ⓦ** website address **ⓔ** email
ⓛ opening times **ⓝ** public transport connections **ⓘ** important

The following symbols are used on the maps:

𝑖 information office		▪ point of interest
✈ airport		○ city
✚ hospital		○ large town
🛡 police station		○ small town
🚌 bus station		═ motorway
✉ post office		─ main road
🚆 railway station		─ minor road
✝ cathedral		─ railway
P+🚆 Park & Ride		

❶ numbers denote featured cafés, restaurants & venues

PRICE CATEGORIES

The ratings below indicate average price rates for a double room per night, including breakfast:

£ under £70 **££** £70–150 **£££** over £150

The typical cost for a three-course meal without drinks is as follows:

£ under £20 **££** £20–30 **£££** over £30

▶ *The Eastgate Clock, England's second most photographed timepiece*

3 8002 01745 150 3

...blished
...brands,
...n travel.

For more than 135 years our
guidebooks have unlocked the secrets
of destinations around the world,
sharing with travellers a wealth of
experience and a passion for travel.

**Rely on Thomas Cook as your
travelling companion on your next trip
and benefit from our unique heritage.**

Thomas Cook **pocket** guides

CHESTER

2 4 APR 2017

Your travelling companion since 1873

Written by David Cawley

Published by Thomas Cook Publishing
A division of Thomas Cook Tour Operations Limited
Company registration no. 3772199 England
The Thomas Cook Business Park, Unit 9, Coningsby Road,
Peterborough PE3 8SB, United Kingdom
Email: books@thomascook.com, Tel: +44 (0) 1733 416477
www.thomascookpublishing.com

Produced by Cambridge Publishing Management Limited
Burr Elm Court, Main Street, Caldecote CB23 7NU
www.cambridgepm.co.uk

ISBN: 978-1-84848-486-3

This first edition © 2011 Thomas Cook Publishing
Text © Thomas Cook Publishing
Cartography supplied by Redmoor Design, Tavistock, Devon
Map data © OpenStreetMap contributors CC-BY-SA, www.openstreetmap.org,
www.creativecommons.org

Series Editor: Karen Beaulah
Production/DTP: Steven Collins

Printed and bound in Spain by GraphyCems

Cover photography © Jon Arnold Images Ltd/Alamy

All rights reserved. No part of this publication may be reproduced, stored in
any retrieval system or transmitted, in any form or by any means, electronic,
mechanical, recording or otherwise, in any part of the world, without prior
permission of the publisher. Requests for permission should be made to the
publisher at the above address.

Although every care has been taken in compiling this publication, and the contents
are believed correct at the time of printing, Thomas Cook Tour Operations
Limited cannot accept any responsibility for errors or omissions, however caused,
or for changes in detail given in this guide, or for the consequences of any
reliance on the information provided. Descriptions and assessments are based on
the author's views and experience when writing and do not necessarily represent
those of Thomas Cook Tour Operations Limited.

Coventry City
Council

EAR

3 8002 01745 150 3	
Askews & Holts	May-2011
914.271404	£3.99
CB 29/05/11	

INTRODUCING
Chester

Introduction

Chester is undeniably a gem of a European destination. It's a condensed cache of history, culture and distinctive retail, all tightly corseted by beautifully preserved stone walls enveloping a city that's clung on through the ravages of war, plague and post-war brutalist modernism to preserve its unique character and charm. Proving that size certainly isn't everything, its diminutive, must-see cosmopolitan nucleus certainly packs an imperial punch well above its weight when it comes to things to do, see and enjoy.

Coveted by the Romans, Chester has spent the following two millennia developing itself into an absorbing, stylish place that has continually beguiled visitors during the ebb and flow of its long and rich history. Even for visitors less absorbed with the past, Chester's magnetism comes with one of the best and most unusual shopping experiences in the kingdom among its multi-tiered **Rows**. The city has a glorious riverside setting and a series of highly regarded annual festivals and events, complemented by a nightlife and restaurant scene to keep its peers and bigger city neighbours permanently on their toes. Style and history seamlessly blend together, while in recent years the characters of the soap opera *Hollyoaks* have further raised the profile of the city.

With a permanent population of over 118,000, bolstered by an annual influx of around 8,000 students, Cheshire's capital and centre for legal and financial services is well connected in every respect. And, when busy city street life gets a little too much, both rural and coastal alternatives are just a short journey beyond its walls. Surrounding **Cheshire** offers rich, gentle rolling countryside sprinkled with prosperous villages and sights of interest, while for some, the handsome, fun and increasingly back-in-vogue resort of **Llandudno** and its breathtaking bay of myth and legend offer a perfect antidote.

For a city so small, Chester is packed to its famous barricades with enthralling elegance and splendour. Here, the old encompasses the new, and tucked around every historic street corner an unexpected treasure can be found.

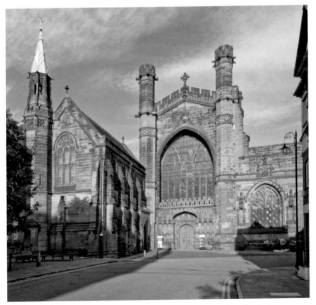

⬤ *Pagan places of worship lie at the same spot as Chester's cathedral*

When to go

SEASONS & CLIMATE

Like all other British cities, Chester is very much in the hands of the gods when it comes to weather. While there is never a bad time to visit, spring and summer, when the average temperature climbs to around 21°C (70°F), are overwhelmingly the most pleasant seasons to be there. The climate tends to be drier and the already busy streets come alive to the sights and sounds of street entertainers and festivals. This is also the best time for those who want to explore on foot the gorgeous Cheshire countryside or the seaside delights of Llandudno. But even at the height of summer, shrewd travellers carry a waterproof.

ANNUAL EVENTS

Chester packs in an eclectic collection of cerebral and just plain fun happenings throughout the year. From May to September, **Chester Racecourse** hosts all kinds of equine activities at its famous and historic course, which is set in beautiful surroundings close by the city walls (see page 21). During the summer months, the **Festival of Chester** brings together a variety of popular events including the **Roman Festival** and **Midsummer Watch Parade** (ⓦ www.visitchester.com), while Screen Deva is a 10-day celebration of film and digital media presentations hosted in a collection of often unusual venues (ⓦ www.chesterperforms.com). **Chestival** is 34 days and nights of family-friendly fun, complemented by the highly regarded choral and classical music of the **Summer Music Festival**.

Those who prefer their tunes a little more bass pounding should visit Chester during the August bank holiday **Creamfields** festival (Ⓦ www.creamfields.com).

In the autumn, during England's biggest and free celebration of local architecture, culture and history, the **Heritage Open Days** provide access to some of the city's star historic buildings (Ⓦ heritageopendayschester.co.uk) while the **Literature Festival** showcases established and new writers during two weeks of celebrations.

The onset of **Christmas** brings out the best of the city's historic streets with a whole host of festive happenings, including the loud and colourful **Winter Watch Parade** (first two Thursdays in December). For listings of events throughout the year visit Ⓦ www.chesterfestivals.co.uk

○ *The Museum Gardens are a treasure trove of Roman architectural remains*

History

England's past in a microcosm, Chester's beautifully preserved and still emerging archaeology reflects every famous period of the country's history from its beginnings some 2,000 years ago. In AD 75, Chester lay on the very edge of the known world. The Romans first saw the potential of this large raised spit of land, partially encircled by a broad galleon-friendly River Dee, one of the largest fortresses in Britain. Named **Deva** (pronounced *day wah*), the country's largest fortress and adjoining supply town were to play a major role as a trading centre and base for the colonisation of northern *Britannia*. Wines and oils were imported from the Mediterranean, while wild bears, copper and silver were just some of the local indigenous specialities taken back to Rome for its imperial amusement and expansion.

Following the Roman abandonment of Britain around AD 410, the city plunged into the Dark Ages only to resurrect itself 600 years later as a principal market town and port following a series of cross-border skirmishes and shifts of power with its Welsh neighbours. The 11th century brought mixed fortunes at the hands of the conquering Norman forces who were responsible for both devastating destruction and rebuilding and cultural renaissance. We have this period to thank for many of the attractions still visited today. The Middle Ages were also a defining time for the thriving city. Traders produced and sold their goods from newly created cellars and balconies in the beginnings of the city's now famous shopping **Rows**. Despite losing its shipping port to silt and getting battered, bruised and decimated by both the English Civil War (1642–51) and several outbreaks of plague, Chester overcame the crises. It expanded through the 18th and 19th centuries as a place of commerce and as a fashionable Victorian resort, where promenading back and forward atop the Roman-conceived city walls became quite the thing to do. Today, still surrounded by reminders of its long and illustrious past, Chester continues to thrive as a destination for both business visitors drawn to its large financial and legal sector and leisure trippers captivated by its matchless retail and historic attractions.

Chester's hidden gem: the 17th-century Alms Houses on Park Street

Culture

Chester has engaging fine museums, with the **Grosvenor Museum** (see page 59) bringing the city's past and present to life through a regularly changing programme of fine, modern and decorative arts alongside its compelling interpretations of the area's history and heritage. **The Dewa Roman Experience** (see page 58) exposes and recreates the life and times of Roman Chester, while the **Cheshire Military Museum** (see page 58) depicts the army regiments connected with the county. The city also has some first-rate private galleries peppered across the centre, but it is music where Chester really comes into its own, with the highly esteemed choral and orchestral **Summer Music Festival** (ⓦ www.chesterfestivals.co.uk). The **cathedral** also plays host to a number of concerts throughout the year, including performances by the **Chester Philharmonic Orchestra**. Jazz, too, plays a big part in the city's fabric with a host of venues offering everything from the laid back to the most baffling, while **Chester Performs** takes to the greenery of **Grosvenor Park** to offer some much vaunted open-air theatre performances (ⓦ www.chesterperforms.com).

● *Chester's tower offers splendid views of the city*

✓ MAKING THE MOST OF
Chester

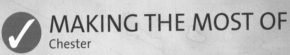

Shopping

The number of well-turned-out shoppers, their fingers straining around handles of heavy high-class designer carrier bags, tells you that this is a place that takes the art of shopping extremely seriously. The Chester retail experience is without doubt extremely rewarding, where even the most battle-hardened shopaholic will find something completely new to experience. Even those who see shopping as nothing more than a chore will not fail to be enchanted and intrigued by the medieval and Victorian shop architecture.

As on all other British high streets, outlets of the major retail chains are on hand, but what separates this city from the homogenised shopping experience in so many towns – apart from the unique buildings – is the excellent collection of independent retailers. **Northgate**, **Eastgate**, **Bridge Street** and **Watergate Street** all host the famous shopping Rows that have made this a prized place to venture and hit the plastic. Hidden pleasures can be found in **Rufus Court** and along **Godstall Lane** while the **Grosvenor Shopping Centre** offers high-end retail outlets including landmark department store **Browns** (now run by Debenhams). The city has also earned itself quite a reputation as an antiques centre with the famous Bonham's auctioneers having a presence among the large collection of art, jewellery and furnishings specialists found throughout the city centre.

For cheap and cheerful shopping, Chester **Indoor Market** and the attached **Forum Shopping Centre** trade in fresh local produce and the day-to-day necessities of life.

Christmas is a further bonus to the overall retail magnetism and a particularly magical time for shopping in the city. Early November sees the city illuminated beneath a blanket of dazzling lights while traders bring their stalls to the streets and squares, creating a joyously traditional and festive atmosphere.

● *The Rows are both shopping heaven and architectural treat*

Eating & drinking

As should be anticipated in such a high-profile and affluent city, the array of places to nibble and gorge is ample, ranging from Michelin-starred restaurants to fast-food joints and from gastro pubs to old-time boozers serving traditional hearty pies and stews served with mounds of potatoes and vegetables. With local Cheshire dairy products very much a part of the food heritage, that quintessential British pastime of afternoon cream teas is another well-respected tradition in these parts, served up in the late afternoon in Chester's many cafés and hotels. The surrounding county's fertile soil makes for some excellent locally produced apples, strawberries, asparagus and potatoes, while nearby rich forests help to sustain a supply of some fine seasonal game. Cheshire cheeses, Welsh lamb and seafood sourced straight from the nearby Irish Sea and seasoned by salt from Cheshire's famous saline pans all help chefs work their magic in Chester's kitchens.

For DIY alfresco dining, the city offers a choice of places to grab all the ingredients necessary for a picnic and a selection of tranquil scenes in which to enjoy it, including the **Grosvenor** and **Queens Parks**, the riverside, the **Memorial Garden**, **cloister garden** and **Cathedral Square**.

Lovers of both grape and grain will have no difficulty in finding a place to slake their thirsts, with a wealth of wine bars and historic pubs offering a dazzling array of real ales, including Chester's very own 'Spitting Feathers' and 'WC Brewery'. To get a full appreciation of what the city and its county have to offer, a series of taste trails has been devised offering visitors the chance to understand more about the region's fare while of course enjoying the odd sample along the way ( www.tastecheshire.com). Lunch is usually served between 12.00 and 14.00 with dinner service generally from 18.00 until 21.30.

The Albion has kept its quirky, traditional look and feel

Entertainment

Come the weekend, Chester's streets enjoy a short lull before filling again with a healthy collection of vivacious young and old things. Chester's nightlife is equally vibrant and almost as varied as its bigger near-neighbours, Liverpool and Manchester. Having a university within walking distance helps the revelry along in eye-wateringly cool wine bars and time-honoured hostelries that have been pulling pints for the past 500 years.

Cinemagoers will find a mainstream, multiscreen cinema complex to the west of the city (ⓐ Greyhound Retail Park, Sealand Road ❶ 0871 200 2000 Ⓦ www.cineworld.co.uk), while the **Chester Film Society** presents more international and independent offerings in three venues across the city centre (Ⓦ www.chesterfilmfans.co.uk).

Unusually for a place of its status, Chester citizens don't have a major theatre at the moment, though they do have the **Forum Studio Theatre**, home to resident amateur but very proficient theatre company, **Tip Top Theatre Productions** (see pages 48–9). For professional productions, a journey to Manchester or Liverpool or even across the border into Wales is required. Both the **Venue Cymru** in Llandudno (ⓐ The Promenade, Llandudno ❶ 01492 872000 Ⓦ www.venuecymru.co.uk) and the **Clwyd Theatr Cymru** (ⓐ Mold ❶ 0845 330 3565 Ⓦ www.clwyd-theatr-cymru.co.uk) host regular programmes of top touring shows, concerts and drama.

Back on the city streets of Eastgate, Watergate and The Groves, performers continue the centuries-old tradition of entertaining passers-by with a mixture of sometimes questionable, sometimes gifted talents. Information on entertainment can be sought in Visit Chester's monthly and free *What's On* magazine, which is placed in pubs, restaurants and bars across the city, or from its website (ⓦ www.visitcheshire. com). You can also call into the **Chester Tourist Information Centre** at the Town Hall (see page 93), where tickets can also be bought. Those looking for classical, operatic, jazz and folk performance listings should go to ⓦ www.musicinchester.co.uk

🔺 *Aspiring musicians entertaining the crowds on Eastgate*

Sport & relaxation

PARTICIPATION SPORTS
Aquatic sports

Those who enjoy aquatic activities should make their way to Llandudno on the Welsh coast for some sailing, windsurfing, diving and sea fishing exhilaration (see page 80).

Golf

Golfers have a gamut of challenges, including **Chester Golf Club** (ⓐ Curzon Park North ⓣ 01244 677760 ⓦ www.chestergc. co.uk), which offer an unrivalled par-71 setting. For a more informal experience, the municipal **Westminster Park Golf Club** offers nine holes for all ages and levels. ⓐ Hough Green ⓣ 01244 680231.

Walking and cycling

Inland, the **Delamere Forest** has a host of rural walking, cycling and riding trails (see page 87), all just a short distance from the city. Back in Chester, Grosvenor Park, Queens Park, The Groves on the banks of the Dee and indeed the racecourse itself (when not being pounded by horses) make ideal spots for some gentle contemplative ambling.

SPECTATOR SPORTS
Basketball

'Tipping-off' in September, basketball fans will find the **Cheshire Jets** just outside the city walls. ⓐ Northgate Arena ⓣ 01244 302 010 ⓦ www.jetsbasketball.co.uk Ⓝ Bus: 1, 3, 10 ⓘ Admission charge

Football

Those in need of a live football fix should offer much-needed support to perennial strugglers **Chester FC** ⓐ Deva Stadium, Bumpers Lane ⓣ 01244 371376 ⓦ www.chester-city.co.uk ⓝ Bus: 6,10,13 ⓘ Admission charge

Racing

Mention sport and Chester in the same sentence and horse racing is sure to be the common denominator. **Chester Racecourse** (ⓐ New Crane Street ⓣ 01244 304600 ⓦ www.chester-races.co.uk ⓘ Admission charge) is the country's oldest and indeed one of its most picturesque. Set by the city walls, this is home to a series of weekend equestrian events that include polo and show jumping.

▲ *Don your Sunday best and spend an unforgettable day at the races*

Accommodation

Given its popularity as a tourist and retail destination, Chester offers plenty of choice when it comes to resting weary limbs, especially within and around the city walls and beyond the long and leafy Hoole Road, some 15–20 minutes' walk from the centre. From grand 5-star hotels to more modest homely guesthouses, and from swanky boutiques to hostels, the city provides something for all budgets and tastes. These choices however can be limited, particularly during race meetings. If your visit coincides with such an event, you would be well advised to book in advance; a speculative arrival without a reservation may lead to disappointment. If such circumstances are unavoidable, head to the **Chester Tourist Information Centre** (see page 93) and the staff will be happy to find you a bed for the night.

HOTELS

ABode ££ Close to all the shopping districts and attractions, the latest addition to this small sophisticated hotel chain offers style and the latest in pampering and gadgetry. You also get wonderful views of the city, racecourse and hills beyond. A gym, 5th-floor bar and underground parking are also included, and if expenses or budget allow, go for one of the 6th-floor suites. ⓐ Grosvenor Road ⓣ 01244 347000 ⓦ www.abodehotels.co.uk/chester

Best Western Premier Queen Hotel ££ Opposite the railway station, this grand old Victorian dame has quite prestigious names in its guest book; Lillie Langtree and Charles Dickens were just two of the regular guests. Many of the original fine decoration has been sympathetically incorporated into its modern decor and facilities. **ⓐ** City Road **ⓣ** 01244 305000 **ⓦ** www.bw-queenhotel.co.uk

Grosvenor Pulford Hotel & Spa ££ Just a short journey south of the city and set in its own manicured grounds, this country house retreat combines old world charm with 21st-century technology and pampering. Rooms are colourful and both the extensive spa and European-themed restaurant have earned themselves quite a reputation with guests and award nominators. **ⓐ** Wrexham Road, Pulford **ⓣ** 01244 570560 **ⓦ** www.grosvenorpulfordhotel.co.uk

Mill Hotel & Spa ££ This lively 129-bed hotel recreated from a former mill building just outside the city walls features a choice of restaurants, swimming pool, gym, sauna, steam room and spa, as well as boasting its own canal cruiser offering a range of excursions. **ⓐ** Milton Street **ⓣ** 01244 350035 **ⓦ** www.millhotel.com

Chester Grosvenor & Spa £££ Very much part of the fabric of the city, the North West's only red five-star hotel has been a grand bastion of grace and sophistication for 150 years. The 80 unique bedrooms and suites all come with indulgences, space and taste, while the spa offers an array of exclusive treatments for mind, body and soul. **ⓐ** Eastgate **ⓣ** 01244 324024 **ⓦ** www.chestergrosvenor.com

Green Bough Hotel £££ You will find this multi-award-winning, elegant town house just a short journey from the city centre. Each of the 15 rooms is individually designed in a winning fusion of traditional and modern styles. Dining is provided by the Olive Tree restaurant and includes a rooftop garden.
ⓐ 60 Hoole Road ⓣ 01244 326241
ⓦ www.chestergreenboughhotel.com

GUESTHOUSES

Grove Villa £ Just a short stroll from the city centre, this small but perfectly formed guesthouse offers three rooms right on the banks of the River Dee. Period Victorian furniture adds to the charm and a selection of riverside restaurants can be found nearby. ⓐ 18 The Groves ⓣ 01244 349 713
ⓦ www.grovevillachester.com

Mitchell's of Chester £ Acclaimed 5-star guesthouse in a large sympathetically restored Victorian residence set in its own compact landscaped gardens among the city's southern suburbs. The owners' friendliness and breakfasts are just part of the appeal. ⓐ 28 Hough Green ⓣ 01244 679004
ⓦ www.mitchellsofchester.com

Ba Ba Guesthouse ££ Nicely decorated family-run guesthouse on the leafy Hoole Road, east of the city's attractions, offering all the standard in-room facilities but with the bonus of free Wi-Fi. A two-bedroom self-catering apartment is also available. ⓐ 65 Hoole Road ⓣ 01244 315047
ⓦ www.babaguesthouse.co.uk

Chester Recorder House ££ Although located in the heart of the city, this splendid Georgian guesthouse is tucked away in a tranquil elevated position overlooking the river away from the hubbub. Named after star signs, rooms are individually and beautifully decorated, and many of them come with four-poster beds. ⓐ 19 City Walls ⓣ 01244 326580 ⓦ www.recorderhotel.co.uk

HOSTELS

Chester Backpackers £ Close to both the railway station and all the fun and sights of the city centre, this hostel offers plenty of facilities including en-suite rooms, free Wi-Fi, tours desk, washing and kitchen facilities together with a TV lounge for guests. There is 24-hour access and a free left-luggage facility. ⓐ 67 Boughton ⓣ 01244 400185 ⓦ www.chesterbackpackers.co.uk

CAMPING AND CARAVANNING

Chester Fairoaks £ Run by the Caravan Club, this oak-tree-bounded caravan and campsite offers plenty of facilities as befits its 5-star status. Welcoming and family friendly, its location next to a major road means that the sights and shopping in and around Chester are only a short journey away. ⓐ Rake Lane, Little Stanney ⓣ 01513 551600 ⓦ www.caravanclub.co.uk ⓝ Bus: 4, 4X

Southerly Touring Park £ Located 5 km (3 miles) to the south of Chester, this spacious site accommodates caravans, tents and motor homes. It has showers, a shop and a children's play area. ⓐ Balderton Lane, Marlston Cum Lache ⓣ 01244 671308 ⓦ www.chestersoutherly.co.uk

THE BEST OF CHESTER

Surprisingly for a popular city with historic importance and status, Chester is not overly endowed with high-profile museums and galleries. That said, the city still has a wide variety of places to marvel at and enjoy.

TOP 10 ATTRACTIONS

- **The Rows** Arguably the city's biggest pull, this fine collection of historic galleries and cellars hosting shops and bars is unique in the world (see page 48).

- **Chester races** One of the most attractive and unusual courses in the country, Chester holds a series of races and events (see page 70).

- **Chester Cathedral** With over a thousand years of history, this cathedral stands testament to the dedication and the skilled artisanship of its creators (see pages 46–8).

- **Chester Zoo** The UK's foremost charity zoo plays host to over 7,000 rare, exotic and endangered species (see pages 70–72).

- **Dewa Roman Experience** A fascinating study of both local Roman history and archaeology in the city (see page 58).

- **Grosvenor Museum** Chester's long history brought to life over several floors accompanied by a small art gallery (see page 59).

- **River cruise** A chance to witness the city and lovely surrounding countryside from the historic tranquillity of the Dee (see pages 68–9).

- **Walking the Walls** Free to follow, the UK's most complete ancient city wall offers historical insights and marvellous views of the city (see page 30).

- **Llandudno** One of the UK's greatest and most attractive seaside resorts offers all kinds of fun and dramatic seaside splendour in equal measures (see pages 80–83).

- **Vale Royal** (mid-Cheshire) Rich, verdant landscapes surround picturesque well-to-do villages and a host of sights to enjoy (see pages 84–8).

⊘ Archaeological excavations behind the Amphitheatre

Suggested itineraries

HALF-DAY: CHESTER IN A HURRY

When time is limited, head first to the phenomenon that is the **Rows**, in the heart of the city, for a cursory look at its collection of unique shops, bars and restaurants. Next climb the stone steps on to the walls at **Eastgate Clock** and make the two-hour circuitous walk around the ancient walls for a splendid panorama of the city past and present.

1 DAY: TIME TO SEE A LITTLE MORE

A full day means every nook and cranny of the Rows and its retail opportunities can be enjoyed at leisure, including breaks for weary limbs in a choice of historic cafés and restaurants hidden in its cellars and galleries. When shopping has run its course, head to the nearby soaring **cathedral** for some cathartic peace and the grandiose spectacle of dedication and worship. If time allows, pick up the open-top bus tour of the city.

2–3 DAYS: SHORT CITY BREAK

A short break offers all the time that should be needed to fully do the city justice as well as experience its fine choice of restaurants and nightlife. To get an overview of the city make for the **Chester Tourist Information Centre** (see page 93) to join one of the many themed walking tours, such as History, Secret Chester, The Rows, Food and Drink and, come the evening, Ghost Trails. Head as well to the collections found at the **Dewa Roman Experience**, **Cheshire Military Museum** and the **Grosvenor Museum and Art Gallery**. A riverboat tour on the Dee is a good way to catch one's breath and ease tired feet. Outside the centre, almost a full day is needed to do justice to walking and talking with the animals at **Chester Zoo**.

LONGER: ENJOYING CHESTER TO THE FULL

With the luxury of time, all the attractions and sights of Chester and the surrounding area are at your feet. Satisfied that you have exhausted all the city has to offer, make the short journey to the Welsh coast to spend some time at the wonderful and once-again fashionable resort of **Llandudno**. Alternatively, head inland to the charming Cheshire countryside to explore some lovely rural scenery peppered with rustically charming villages that hide some surprising and curious sights.

● *Spend a sunny day at the Groves (see page 30)*

Something for nothing

Simply ambling along **The Groves** on the north bank of the river and the **city walls**, stopping at the various information points and among the city's ancient streets is a compelling wallet-friendly experience. Somewhat off the tourist beat on unremarkable Hamilton Square are the enclosed remnants of the **Roman Treasury**, where garrison soldiers kept both their wages and savings. The **museum gardens** and **Amphitheatre**, too, offer a wealth of Roman architecture (see page 73), while a small collection of archaeological finds can also be found housed outside the **ABode Hotel and HQ building** on Grosvenor Road. Chester is also rich in medieval buildings and one hidden gem is the row of 17th-century **alms houses** found on Park Street. During the summer another attraction takes to the High Cross, when the **town crier** makes daily proclamations to the city folk (see page 45).

EASTGATE CLOCK

The most recognisable landmark in Chester and reputed to be the second most photographed clock in the UK after Westminster, it was commissioned and erected to celebrate the 1897 Diamond Jubilee of Queen Victoria. Perched astride the eastern gateway to the city, public opinion was originally split on its unveiling with some believing it to be whimsical or even too gaudy for its surroundings.

When it rains

Like much of Britain, and its northwest in particular, rain is very much a part of everyday life in Chester, whatever the time of year. Apart from the listings of activities already included, there are also one or two other alternative and rewarding places to seek temporary cover, such as the Rows, which provide a free and unique sheltering solution and some fine shopping on their upper levels.

Back down on street level, the unlikely venue of **Spud-U-Like** (ⓐ 39 Bridge Street ⓣ 01244 311798 ⓞ 09.00–18.00 Mon–Sat, 11.00–17.00 Sun) provides not only dry shelter and hot potato sustenance but comes with a rather unusual attraction. Customers can venture down into the shop's cellar to witness the remnants of the partially revealed Roman hypocaust system that helped to keep the city's influential founding fathers warm and dry during the inclement weather of 1,700 years ago.

Just beyond the city walls, next to Grosvenor Park is another gem worthy of exploration. **St John the Baptist Church** is generally considered one of the finest and most important parish churches in the whole of England. As well as offering a sanctuary for spiritual peace and reflection, it comes with some fine ecclesiastical architecture. St John's also has a long and illustrious musical heritage and even has its own orchestra that, along with other performers, produces some exquisite lunchtime recitals for the public between May and September. When the clouds do part, the former ruins next door of its much bigger and earlier incarnation as a Norman cathedral can be explored. ⓐ Vicar's Lane/Little St John Street ⓣ 01244 403634 ⓦ www.parishofchester.com

On arrival

ARRIVING
By air
Chester does have an airport (Ⓦ www.chesterairport.co.uk) to call its own; however, only travellers privileged and well-heeled enough to have access to a private jet or helicopter can take advantage of it. Instead, the vast majority of visitors choosing to fly here commercially employ the more customary **Liverpool John Lennon Airport** or **Manchester International** (see page 90). People who are concerned about the contribution of air travel to CO_2 emissions that cause climate change can opt to lessen the impact of their flight through **Climate Care** (Ⓦ www. jpmorganclimatecare.com). This site provides comprehensive details on offsetting your CO_2 and the work done on helping environmental projects around the world.

By rail
Many travellers use the train; the city is well served by direct train services from Britain's major cities including London (see page 90). The station is located outside the city walls to the east. It takes 10 minutes to reach the city centre on foot or you can choose to take a taxi or one of the free buses that connect to the city centre bus exchange located by the town hall (see pages 37–8).

By road
Arriving by road is a relatively straightforward affair with an outer and inner ring road delivering you close to points around

the compact centre. It can be a little problematic driving to your ultimate destination, owing to a one-way system and access regulations that can bamboozle even those with satnav. The heart of the city is predominantly pedestrianised and open only to commercial and public transport traffic during the day, although with the arrival of evening these restrictions do lighten up.

Parking places in the centre are fairly plentiful – the short-stay car parks on Princess Street, Trinity Street and Newgate Street and the long-stay car park on Frodsham Street are the most centrally located. Free but limited disabled parking is available at Hamilton Place and Frodsham Street car park for those with appropriate badges. Street parking is extremely limited during weekdays and those planning to stay the night should contact their hotels for parking advice. An alternative is to take advantage of the free parking available at one of four Park & Ride schemes situated at all four points of the compass around the city (see page 90).

FINDING YOUR FEET

This being England, and northern England at that (with Wales nearby), the citizens here are overwhelmingly friendly and helpful and will be more than happy to help you with advice or directions.

That said, like other major tourist destinations, visitors do attract criminals and petty 'ne'er-do-wells' to its crowded streets, who often come from beyond the area to pick the pockets of the unprepared and distracted. A small number of homeless people on the streets ask for spare change, but in general they tend to be quiet, polite and not intimidating.

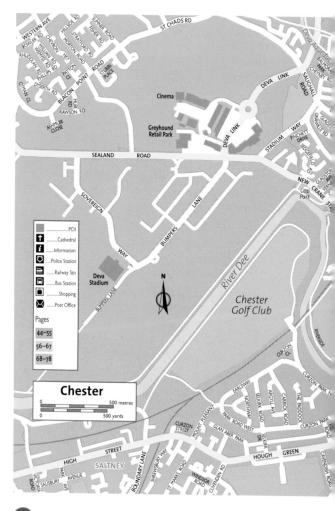

Chester

0 _____ 500 metres

0 _____ 500 yards

Legend:
- POI
- Cathedral
- Information
- Police Station
- Railway Stn
- Bus Station
- Shopping
- Post Office

Pages
44–55
56–67
68–78

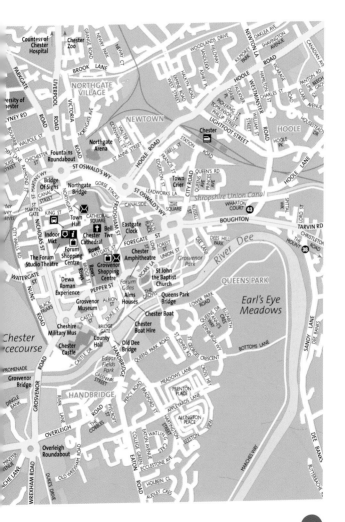

Chester's very compact centre is completely enclosed by its historic wall, making it difficult to wander off course. There are inevitably a few small pockets of less than wholesome districts inside the city walls that add little to the normal visitor experience. As always, human instincts can be quite a reliable indicator as to any clear and present menaces and if they tell you that somewhere or somebody doesn't feel right then they are always best acted upon.

Cheshire Constabulary (see page 91) is responsible for policing, and the city has no more difficulties with crime and safety than any of its similarly sized counterparts.

ORIENTATION

On foot, Chester's compact nature and the legacy of major Roman streets laid out in a grid pattern make it easy to find your way around. The completely encircling walls, inner ring road and River Dee to the south also act as good indicators that the city-centre boundaries have been reached.

Congregating in the predominantly pedestrian-friendly centre, almost all the attractions, sights, shops, bars and restaurants are within these constructed and natural borders. The topography is level around the cathedral, Watergate Street and Eastgate Street areas, south of which the land slopes down to the riverside.

It should take no more than 15 minutes at a gentle pace and without distraction to walk from north to south, and 10 minutes on foot to travel east to west.

GETTING AROUND
By bus

Without a tram or underground metro, public transport is left to buses to circle the city centre. The Bus Exchange on Princess Street (off Northgate Street) is the hub for services in the city centre and to the suburbs and beyond. Many of the buses are low-floor and wheelchair accessible, and the protocol for taking a bus journey is the same here as in the rest of the UK. Simply raise an arm to signal to the driver that you want to board, and when you get on, state your destination and what sort of ticket you need (single, return, day pass etc). It's cash only and the correct change is generally appreciated. It should be noted that there are a number of different bus companies operating in and

● *The Italianate front of Chester railway station*

out of the city, primarily **Arriva** (Ⓦ www.arrivabus.co.uk) and **First** (Ⓦ www.firstgroup.com), and tickets are not necessarily transferable between them.

A **free bus service** is available every 10 minutes (every 20 minutes on Sunday) to valid train ticket holders between the railway station and Frodsham Street in the city centre (Bus: City Rail Link Ⓛ 07.30–19.30 Mon–Sat, Bus: 53 Sun only). For detailed information on all services, including timetables and route finders, contact **Traveline** (Ⓣ 0871 200 2233 Ⓦ www.traveline-northwest.co.uk). Alternatively, call in at the **Chester Tourist Information Centre** (see page 93) or the Public Transport kiosk at the Bus Exchange.

Details of day and weekly passes, along with discounts for students, can be sought from Ⓣ 08708 500868 Ⓦ www.firstgroup.com Ⓛ Ticket Office: 08.30–16.30 daily

Taxis

There are two taxi options in the city. Hackney carriages (black cabs) are plentiful and can be beckoned on the street or boarded from taxi ranks. From north to south, 24-hour ranks can be found outside the railway station, Princess Street/Northgate Street, Foregate and Bridge Streets. They can also be booked in advance Ⓣ 01244 312222. Private mini-cab firms also have a large presence, though these by law cannot collect passengers at random and must be booked in advance.

Abbey Taxis Ⓣ 01244 318318 Ⓦ www.abbeytaxis.net

CSM Ⓣ 0800 44 88871 Ⓦ www.csm-private-hire.com

KingKabs Ⓣ 01244 343434 Ⓦ www.kingkabs.co.uk

Cycling

Chester is a cycle-friendly city with cycle lanes and specific parking facilities including lockers. Popular trails include the towpath beside the Shropshire Union Canal, along the River Dee and the route to Chester Zoo. Route maps for all ages and abilities are available from the Chester Tourist Information Centre (see page 93) or can be downloaded from either ⓦ www.chestercyclecity.org or ⓦ www.cyclechester.com

⬥ Colourful rhinos dot the city

You can hire bikes from **Chester Cycle Hire**, which is located just outside the city centre and has cycles for all shapes and sizes together with the necessary equipment. These can be hired from around £12 per day. ⓐ Strathearn Guesthouse, 38 Hoole Road ⓣ 01244 321522 ⓦ www.chestercyclehire.com

Car hire

Hiring a car is superfluous if you are not planning to journey too far beyond Chester's compact city centre, besides which parking can be a major issue at the best of times. If public transport isn't practical, renting a car might be considered for getting into the surrounding suburbs and countryside. Costs and terms do vary, but a ballpark figure for one day's rental on a four-door intermediate class vehicle should be between £45 and £55. (If planning to hire a car it is worth noting that some companies insist on two domestic utility bills as proof of address and identity along with all parts of the driving licence.)

Avis ⓐ 128 Brook Street ⓣ 0844 581 0014 ⓦ www.avis.co.uk

County Car and Van Hire ⓐ 30 Bumpers Lane ⓣ 01244 383111 ⓦ www.county-rental.co.uk

Enterprise ⓐ Unit 5–6 Hartford Way, Sealand Industrial Estate ⓣ 01244 399393 ⓦ www.enterprise.co.uk

Europcar ⓐ 143 Brook Street ⓣ 01244 588503 ⓦ www.europcar.co.uk

▶ *Watch the world go by on the River Dee*

THE CITY OF
Chester

Introduction to city areas

Comparatively small in size, the centre of Chester has nonetheless been divided into three areas to help make navigating its historic streets and finding its standout attractions, dining and drinking venues an agreeable and straightforward experience.

Two areas within the city centre have been created: City Centre North and City Centre South, divided on a horizontal north–south axis along the continuous major streets of Watergate and Eastgate, with both areas completely encased by the city's surrounding ancient city wall. These two areas host the vast bulk of entertainment and things to see and do.

There is also much to be found in the third area, Outside the City Centre, which covers the broader areas immediately outside the city walls, its leafy suburbs and the nearby surrounding countryside. To access some of the places further afield, public transport or use of a car will be required.

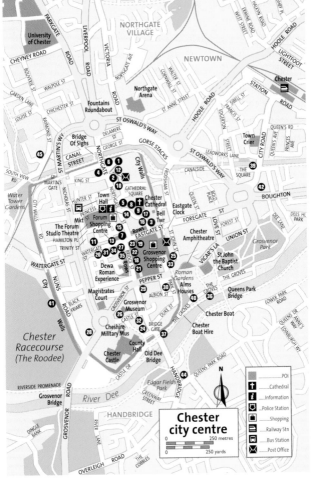

Chester city centre

0 ___ 250 metres
0 ___ 250 yards

POI
Cathedral
Information
Police Station
Shopping
Railway Stn
Bus Station
Post Office

City centre north

Home to the magnificent cathedral, half of the city walls, half of the shopping **Rows** and some fine medieval streets, this area tends to be the business and municipal side of Chester as well as being home to the main **Chester Tourist Information Centre** (see page 93), Bus Exchange and the banks.

SIGHTS & ATTRACTIONS

Chester Cathedral

The cathedral is a large and quite extraordinary ecclesiastical mixture of the old and new. Pagans, Romans and King Alfred's daughter, Queen Ethelfleda (who built a church here to protect the remains of revered St Werburgh) all founded places of worship here before the current incumbent began to take shape during the 11th century. The following 1,000 years saw many changes with architectural fashion as well as battle damage (some caused by the Luftwaffe) driving alterations to the faces and styles of the structure. Chester Cathedral also rightfully claims that its 14th-century wood carvings found in the choir stalls are the finest to behold in the UK. Alongside this are the most complete monastic cloisters in England, which make an excellent location for some tranquil and contemplative time away from the bustle of the city. The morning is a particularly rewarding time to visit when the sun streams in through the beautiful stained glass of the south windows, the majority of visitors have yet to arrive and the rather splendid café is still quiet (see page 52). ⓐ St Werburgh Street ⓣ 01244 324756

○ *Stunning Chester Cathedral and its gardens*

Ⓦ www.chestercathedral.com Ⓛ 09.00–17.00 Mon–Sat, 13.00–
16.00 Sun ❶ Admission charge

Guided walks

A series of compelling, themed guided tours featuring a
selection of subjects such as Food and Drink, Secret Chester, The
Rows and general historic overviews of the city leave from
outside the Town Hall. Times vary and information and tickets
can be bought from the Chester Tourist Information Centre in
the Town Hall itself (see page 93).

Memorial Garden and bell-tower

A tranquil public place of contemplation planted with the
regimental rose, the garden commemorates those of the
Cheshire Regiment who lost their lives during WWII and is next
door to the Cathedral bell-tower. The first of its kind to be built
in 500 years, this houses 13 bells, some of which date back to the
17th century. ⓐ St Werburgh Street

Northgate Bridge

Mounting the stone steps on the historic walls leads to one of the
highest viewing points of the city centre. Though of an early 19th-
century construction the bridge sits astride the foundations of
both medieval and Roman structures and can be the beginning or
end of a fascinating circuitous walk above and around the city.

Town crier

Chester is the last remaining city in the UK to keep its custom of
daily and fixed location town crier proclamations. The current

incumbents of this historic art are the award-winning husband and wife team David and Julie Mitchell, the world's first married couple to do the job. ⓐ The High Cross 🕐 12.00 Tues–Sat only (May–Aug); Race Days 10.30 (ⓦ www.chester-races.co.uk)

Town hall

A magnificent Gothic structure resplendent in grey and red sandstone, opened in 1869 by the Prince of Wales (later King Edward VII), the town hall is now a popular venue for seminars and civil weddings. Above the main entrance are four sculptures depicting: Roman soldiers building the city walls, Egbert (802–39), King of the West Saxons and conqueror of Mercia (which

⬥ Chester's magnificent Gothic town hall

then included Chester), Charles I's entry to the city in 1642 and William the Conqueror presenting Hugh I with the earldom of the city around 1077. ② Northgate Street

CULTURE

The Forum Studio Theatre

This highly acclaimed, top quality community theatre is in the heart of the city at the former Gateway Theatre. For over 60

THE ROWS

Chester's famous Rows are a striking collection of black and white, half-timbered buildings found in the heart of the city and running along either side of the city's original Roman roads. However, while very much looking like a shopping mall designed by the Tudors, most are in fact a product of the Victorian period built during an era when copying the vernacular in all its art forms was not only in vogue but also a shrewd way of attracting visitors to the city.

Above street level the covered wooden galleries in their original form would have been the location for both stalls and traders' homes while the stone basements would have been ideal for storage. Shoemakers, Cooks and Ironmongers Row give some indication as to the specific trades that once occupied the area, though today no such restrictive demarcations apply, with great shops, bars and eateries of all denominations found on their three levels.

years its resident group, Tip Top Theatre Productions, has been presenting a broad spectrum of affordable and well-received contemporary and classical dramas, comedy and musical productions. **ⓐ** Hamilton Place **ⓣ** 01244 341296 **ⓦ** www.tiptopproductions.co.uk

RETAIL THERAPY

This is home to half of the city's unique and fascinating shopping experience found on its famous **Rows**, which can be found at the southern end of Northgate Street and northern side of Eastgate and Watergate Streets. Exploration around the cathedral also unearths some hidden retail gems. For sports, outdoor wear and unique jewellery, try the small cluster of shops on **Rufus Court** or head to **Godstall Lane** for a small collection of independent fashion shops. The small and functional **Forum Shopping Centre** (**ⓐ** Northgate Street **ⓦ** forumshopping.co.uk **ⓣ** 07.30–18.00 Mon–Sat, 10.00–16.00 Sun) is the place to head for high-street stores such as Boots the Chemist, Somerfield and T J Hughes and is connected to **Chester Market** (**ⓐ** 6 Princess Street **ⓦ** www.chestermarket.com **ⓣ** 08.00–17.00 Mon–Sat, closed Sun) where all kinds of food, homeware and general paraphernalia can be had, often at bargain prices.

TAKING A BREAK

Ceramic Café £ ❶ Combine satisfying your hunger from a choice selection of light snacks and homemade cakes with any spontaneous creative urges. Suitable for all ages and abilities, here you can relax, throw some clay on the wheel and daub some finished pottery. ⓐ Rufus Court ⓣ 01244 345661 ⓦ www.ceramiccafechester.co.uk ⓛ 10.00–17.00 Wed–Sat, 17.30–21.30 Thur adults only, 10.00–16.00 Sun, closed Mon & Tues

The Cheese Shop £ ❷ For takeaway only, here is a spectacular and award-winning collection of over 200 cheese varieties from the cow, goat and ewe as well as selections of pasteurised, unpasteurised and vegetarian varieties. You can buy handmade biscuits, preserves and chutneys to accompany them. Great for a picnic. ⓐ 116 Northgate Street ⓣ 01244 346240

ⓞ *The centre of buzzing Chester at High Cross*

ⓦ www.chestercheeseshop.co.uk ⓒ 08.30–17.30 Mon–Sat, closed Sun

The Cheshire Sandwich Company £ ❸ Tucked down a historic lane, this is a great takeaway for a choice of breakfasts, sandwiches and salads that can be enjoyed on the benches of the nearby and tranquil Memorial Gardens. ⓐ 4 Godstall Lane ⓣ 01244 347339 ⓦ www.cheshiresandwichcompany.co.uk ⓒ 08.30–14.30 Mon–Fri, 08.30–15.00 Sat, closed Sun

Chez Jules £ ❹ Proof that French food need not be intimidatingly expensive; this very popular Parisian-style bistro serves up a healthy dose of fine food and lively *joie de vivre*. Gastro events take place throughout the year with their French regional speciality nights a particular draw. ⓐ 71 Northgate Street ⓣ 01244 400014 ⓦ www.chezjules.com ⓒ 12.00–15.00 & 18.00–22.30 Mon–Fri, 12.00–22.30 Sat, 12.00–16.00 Sun

Funky Cow £ ❺ This modern, upbeat milkshake bar and takeaway serves a rainbow of traditional and bizarre flavours (Marmite anyone?) that can be mixed up any which way you like. Hot chocolate drinks are also a speciality. ⓐ 31 St Werburgh Street ⓣ 01244 351555 ⓔ enquiries@funkycowmilkshakes.co.uk ⓒ 10.00–17.30 Mon–Fri, 10.00–17.00 Sat, 11.00–16.00 Sun

Joseph Benjamin £ ❻ An award-winning combination of restaurant and deli serving up seasonal and locally available produce to create a small but perfectly formed British-inspired menu with contemporary twists. ⓐ 140 Northgate Street

☎ 01244 344295 **ⓦ** www.josephbenjamin.co.uk **🕐** 09.00–17.00 Tues & Wed, 09.00–21.00 Thur–Sat, 10.00–17.00 Sun, closed Mon

Katie's Tea Rooms £ ❼ Harking back to bygone days, this is a quintessential old-fashioned tea shop, which, alongside afternoon tea served on three-tiered cake stands, also offers jacket potatoes, salads and sandwiches – all served by waitresses in maids' uniforms. **ⓐ** 36 Watergate Street **☎** 01244 400322 **ⓦ** www.mdsrestaurant.co.uk **🕐** 10.00–17.00 Wed–Sat, closed Sun–Tues

The Refectory £ ❽ Built in the 13th century as a dining hall for the 40 resident Benedictine monks and the guests of the cathedral. Today, light snacks dominate the menu, and among the splendid surroundings a number of historic features can be admired in the natural light streaming through the stained glass. **ⓐ** Chester Cathedral **☎** 01244 500964 **ⓦ** www.chestercathedral.com **🕐** 09.30–16.30 Mon–Sat, 12.00–16.00 Sun

Sergio's £ ❾ This is one of the city's most celebrated restaurants. Authentic rustic Italian food is backed up by 30 years of family flair and friendliness in informal trattoria surroundings. Pasta and pizza are perennial favourites and there is a healthy dose of attention-grabbing antipasti, meat and fish dishes. **ⓐ** 18a St Werburgh Street **☎** 01244 314663 **ⓦ** www.ristorantesergio.co.uk **🕐** 12.00–15.00 & 18.00–22.00 Sun–Fri, 12.00–22.30 Sat

Taconita £ ❿ This bright, colourful and informal Mexican diner serves up tacos, quesadillas and a selection of traditional hearty favourites. Special offers are available including 'meal deals' and 'all you can eat' Thursdays as well as menus to accompany the open-air concerts that take place in **Rufus Court**. ⓐ 4 Rufus Court ❶ 01244 312191 Ⓦ www.taconita.com 🕐 11.30–16.00 Tues, 11.30–21.00 Wed & Thur, 11.30–22.00 Fri & Sat, 12.00–16.00 Sun, closed Mon

Aquavit ££ ⓫ French and Italian staples with a leftfield twist of Swedish influences dominate the menu in this traditionally presented and low-key eatery that combines contemporary and old-fashioned furnishings to some effect.

🔺 *Head to Northgate for a quick snack or a drawn-out lunch*

ⓐ 58 Watergate Street ⓣ 01244 313721 ⓦ www.
restaurantaquavitus.co.uk ⓛ 12.00–14.45 & 18.00–22.00 Mon–
Sat, closed Sun

AFTER DARK

Alexander's ⑫ Specialising in live jazz, folk, world and comedy
acts, this friendly and popular bar serves international and local
food during the day and early evening. A terrace is occasionally
employed to host outdoor concerts and there is free live jazz on
Sunday afternoons. ⓐ Rufus Court ⓣ 01244 340005
ⓦ www.alexanderslive.com ⓛ 11.00–02.00 Mon–Sat,
12.00–00.30 Sun

Amber Lounge ⑬ Cool, smart and sophisticated, this lounge
bar and restaurant features DJs playing funky, soulful tunes.
One of the most comprehensive cocktail and spirit menus
in the city helps keep things moving among the rich velvet
and wood decor. ⓐ 8 Watergate Row ⓣ 01244 316477
ⓦ www.amberlounge.com ⓛ 11.30–23.30 Mon–Wed,
11.30–01.00 Thur, 11.30–02.00 Fri, 11.00–02.00 Sat,
11.30–00.30 Sun

Babylon ⑭ Remember when Oasis took on Blur, the Spice Girls
championed girl power and Right Said Fred was too sexy for
everything? Music of the 1990s is kept alive and popping in this
bold and brash celebration, which occasionally features live star
performances and guest DJs championing the decade.
ⓐ 12–16 Northgate Street ⓣ 01244 327141 ⓦ www.babylonbars.

co.uk ⏰ 21.00–03.00 Mon–Thur, 21.00–03.30 Fri, 20.00–04.00 Sat, 22.00–03.00 Sun

The Commercial ⑮ A hidden gem of a traditional pub, eatery and hotel. The bar features a warren of small rooms decorated in an eclectic mixture of pop, contemporary and traditional accessories and furnishings. Outside there is a courtyard for some alfresco sipping and nibbling. ⓐ Northgate Street ⓣ 01244 409319 ⓦ www.thecommercialhotelchester.com ⏰ 12.00–02.00 Mon–Sat, 12.00–24.00 Sun

Duttons ⑯ Another destination for Chester's smart set, this comes decorated in exposed brick and dark woods. The bustling Duttons is concealed on one of the city's medieval streets and offers all-day dining until mid-evening, when funky music is cranked up, candles are lit and the wine-bar atmosphere takes hold. Friendly staff and a small terrace at the front add to the appeal. ⓐ 12 Godstall Lane ⓣ 01244 401869 ⓦ www.duttonschester.co.uk ⏰ 10.00–23.00 Sun–Thur, 10.00–01.00 Fri & Sat

The Living Room ⑰ Cool and contemporary, with an occasional dash of decadence; leather booths, sofas and rich woods feature heavily in this local branch of the celebs' favourite Living Room brand. It's spread over three floors of dining and drinking spaces, and includes a piano bar. ⓐ 13 St Werburgh Street ⓣ 01244 405910 ⓦ www.thelivingroom.co.uk ⏰ 11.00–24.00 Mon & Tues, 11.00–01.00 Wed & Thur, 11.00–02.00 Fri & Sat, 11.00–00.30 Sun

City centre south

South of Watergate and Eastgate Streets is where the mass of Chester's attractions, sights and museums can be found along with the bulk of accommodation and the other half of the famous shopping **Rows**.

SIGHTS & ATTRACTIONS

Chester Castle

Now unfortunately open only by appointment, the castle is best viewed from the southern section of the city walls. There is enough of its original 11th-century exterior fabric to get a small sense of this once-impressive Norman bastion that stood guard over the river and city. ⓐ Castle Street ❶ 01829 260464 ⓦ www.english-heritage.org.uk

Chester Heritage Tour

A quite theatrical guided excursion around the city sights aboard a vintage open-top bus that lasts between 35 and 45 minutes. ⓐ Chester Visitors Centre, Vicar's Lane ❶ 0844 585 4144 ⓦ www.chesterheritagetours.co.uk ❶ 10.00–14.00 Mon–Fri, 10.00–15.00 Sat & Sun (summer only) ❶ Cash only. If wishing to pay by card, tickets can be purchased in advance from the city's information centre (see page 93).

Hop On Hop Off Bus Tour

In summer you can take a one-hour open-top double-decker bus tour of the local sights with the option to jump off and rejoin at any time along its route over the following 24 hours. Small discounts are available if combining this trip with a river cruise (see pages 68–9). ⓐ Stops at various locations ⓘ 0844 585 4144 ⓦ www.city-discovery.com ⓛ From 10.00 daily (Apr–Sept) ⓘ Cash only. If wishing to pay by card, tickets can be purchased in advance from the city's information centres (see page 93).

The Three Old Arches
There is no arguing that Chester's strong retail tradition has a particularly long and still vibrant and visible history. Title holder

⬥ Chester's castle and the walls that surround the city

for the most enduring shop is the Three Old Arches, which dates
from the 13th century and is thought to be the oldest shop front
in the country. For much of the 20th century the space was
dedicated to groceries; it then became a department store
owned by that now bygone name Owen Owen. Today it's home
to a furniture retailer. ⓐ 48 Bridge Street

CULTURE

Cheshire Military Museum

Incorporating visual and audio technology, along with hands-on
displays, this family-friendly museum is dedicated to
interpreting Cheshire's military history and the day-to-day lives
of those it has affected over the past 300 years. ⓐ The Castle
ⓣ 01244 327617 ⓦ www.cheshiremilitarymuseum.co.uk
ⓛ 10.00–17.00 daily ⓘ Admission charge

Dewa Roman Experience

Avoiding the high-tech razzmatazz of other museums, this
diminutive and rather neglected attraction introduces visitors to
the Romans in Britain and Chester in particular. The sights,
sounds and smells are recreated in tableaux of imperial street
life and there is a compelling area dedicated to archaeological
excavations that have taken place beneath the building itself.
A room is also set aside for hands-on kids' activities.
ⓐ Pierpoint Lane (off Bridge Street) ⓣ 01244 343407
ⓦ www.dewaromanexperience.co.uk ⓛ 09.00–17.00 Mon–Sat,
10.00–17.00 Sun (Feb–Nov); 10.00–16.00 daily (Dec & Jan)
ⓘ Admission charge

Grosvenor Museum

This small museum, spread over three floors, covers many aspects of Chester life, including the city's long history, and fine and decorative art. There are also galleries dedicated to costume and natural history. An annex chronicles the changing furnishings and fixtures of a local domestic household. ⓐ 27 Grosvenor Street ⓣ 01244 402033 ⓦ www.grosvenormuseum.co.uk ⓒ 10.30–17.00 Mon–Sat, 13.00–16.00 Sun

RETAIL THERAPY

Perhaps even more rewarding than their northern area neighbours, the Rows continue to be the main attraction here with their choice of distinctive, independent and upmarket

● *The Three Old Arches is thought to be the oldest shop front in the country*

retailers spread over three historic tiered levels. Shopping here is also complemented by the **Grosvenor Shopping Centre**. Entered from any one of Eastgate, Bridge or Pepper Streets this is a two-level mixture of swanky and familiar retail brands, with the Bridge Street entrance an especially charming visual experience. ⓐ Newgate Street ⓣ 01244 353065 ⓦ www.thegrosvenorcentre.co.uk ⓛ 09.00–17.30 Mon–Sat, 11.00–17.00 Sun

TAKING A BREAK

Café Rouge £ ⑩ This is one of many pavement cafés that straddle Bridge Street. Its varied menu and friendly staff make it stand out. A choice of British and European breakfasts, baguettes and croques, salads and quiches sit alongside more substantial à la carte and fixed-price daily specials.
ⓐ 29 Bridge Street ⓣ 01244 315626

SONS AND DAUGHTERS OF CHESTER
Household names who hail from the city include 1980s comedians Russ Abbott and Keith Harris (of Orville the Duck fame) and contemporary funny men Jeff Green and Bob Mills. Footballers Michael Owen and Danny Murphy state Chester on their passports, as do screen actor Daniel Craig and horror specialist Emily Booth. The conductor Sir Adrian Boult, weather presenter Helen Willets and football commentator Martin Tyler also have their roots in the city.

Ⓦ www.brasseriegerard.co.uk/chester.asp Ⓛ 09.00–23.00 Mon–Sat, 09.00–22.30 Sun

Café Venue £ ⓳ Situated in a barrel-vaulted crypt, this 13th-century venue is an unusual place to rest weary shopping and sightseeing limbs and take on board a light snack and drink. It is part of the Debenhams store group. Wi-Fi and takeaway are available. Ⓐ 28–30 Eastgate Ⓣ 0844 561 6161 (ext 4) Ⓛ 10.00–17.00 Mon–Fri, 09.00–17.30 Sat, 09.00–16.30 Sun

Fiesta Havana £ ⓴ Tastes of the Caribbean and Iberian peninsula combine in this a vivacious, informal basement restaurant and bar. Selections of tapas and choice selections

🔺 *Pop into the Grosvenor Shopping Centre*

such as fajitas, paella and fiery stews from popular Latin cuisine combine with mojitos and tequila from the substantial drinks list. Live bands and DJs take to the stage at weekends.
ⓐ 39–41 Watergate Street ⓣ 01244 347878 ⓦ www. fiestahavana.com ⓛ food served 12.00–15.00 & 17.00–23.00 Mon, Wed–Fri & Sun, 12.00–20.00 Tues, 12.00–23.00 Sat

O & F £ ㉑ Taking the art of Italian food very seriously, this shop and café brings its ingredients straight from Italy. As well as introducing a series of events, such as make your own pasta, a recently opened candlelit vault is now open on weekend evenings. ⓐ 61 Bridge Street ⓣ 01244 400945 ⓦ www. olioefarina.com ⓛ 09.00–17.30 Mon–Thur, 09.00–21.00 Fri & Sat, 11.00–17.00 Sun

Purely Wicked £ ㉒ This milkshake and smoothie bar offers over 200 varieties of shakes along with the opportunity to create your own concoctions; the Red Bull shake is seemingly a popular pick-me-up on weekend mornings. Hot drinks include a range of sweet-shop-inspired drinking chocolates and mulled wine.
ⓐ 11 Bridge Street ⓣ 01244 346566 ⓛ 09.00–18.00 Mon–Fri, 10.00–18.00 Sat, 11.00–17.00 Sun

The Sushi Bar £ ㉓ An informal and fun basement restaurant, and the only conveyor-belt bar in Cheshire, this offers plenty more than just the standard sushi fare. Rules of engagement are simple: go to the counter, help yourself to a bit of what you fancy from the priced, colour-coded plates individually passing in front of you and, when sated, the staff will add up the plates

and present a bill. Takeaway is available. ⓐ 15 Bridge Street
ⓣ 01244 341555 ⓦ www.thesushibarchester.com
ⓛ 12.00–22.00 Mon–Sat, 12.00–17.00 Sun

Three Kings Tea Rooms £ ㉔ Bygone café charm: cakes, pastries,
savoury snacks and lunches are served on doilies by women in
traditional black and white uniforms. The building has a long
and interesting heritage dating back to its time as a 17th-
century toll house. ⓐ 90–92 Lower Bridge Street ⓣ 01244 317717
ⓦ www.threekingstearooms.com ⓛ 10.00–17.00 daily

Züger's £ ㉕ A Swiss family enterprise offering a tea room and
patisserie experience alongside light bites and heartier fare at
breakfast and lunch, such as Rösti Alpine and Wiener Schnitzel.
The café is licensed and, when the weather is behaving, a

△ *Learn about Chester life at the Grosvenor Museum*

courtyard offers some indulgent alfresco respite. ⓐ Unit 2,
St John Street ⓣ 01244 348041 ⓦ www.zugerstearooms.co.uk
ⓛ 09.00–17.00 Mon–Sat, 10.00–16.00 Sun

Convivio ££ ㉖ Inside a somewhat austere Victorian building
is a choice of either a plush Italian fine dining experience on
the ground floor or a more casual, almost camp gothic café
bar above. The latter is complemented by a large south-facing
terrace which is popular during the best weather. The menu
is comprehensive, and lunch and early-bird specials are
available. ⓐ 29 Grosvenor Street ⓣ 01244 400029
ⓦ www.conviviochester.co.uk ⓛ 12.00–22.00 daily

Moules a Go Go ££ ㉗ Mussels in hefty pots, served in a variety
of ways, and other Gallic specialities, alongside heaps of *frites* in
bright and lively surroundings make this a popular and award-
winning spot for lunch or dinner. Located on the first floor
gallery, booking at the weekend is recommended.
ⓐ 39 Watergate Row ⓣ 01244 348818 ⓦ www.moulesagogo.
co.uk ⓛ 12.00–15.00 & 18.00–22.00 Mon–Fri, 12.00–22.00 Sat,
12.00–21.00 Sun

Michael Caines £££ ㉘ This fifth-floor fine dining experience
and champagne bar greets you with large pop and cinema icon
artwork on the walls and offers some great views of the city and
racecourse next door. The menu comes with a choice of grazing,
à la carte and tasting options served with friendly panache
either among rich velveteen interiors or alfresco on the
sweeping balcony. ⓐ ABode Hotel, Grosvenor Road

① 01244 347000 ⓦ www.michaelcaines.com ⓛ 12.00–14.30 &
18.00–21.30 Mon–Sat, closed Sun

Oddfellows £££ ㉙ Choose to be served in the Pantry, Brasserie
or a private dining area at this truly distinctive place featuring
imaginative menus created to celebrate the best in British
produce. The interiors exhibit an almost surrealist exuberance,
and the poolside Bedouin-inspired tables within the walled
gardens are worth a visit in themselves. ⓐ 20 Lower Bridge
Street ① 01244 400001 ⓦ www.oddfellows.biz ⓛ 12.00–15.00 &
17.00–21.30 Mon–Sat, 12.00–21.00 Sun

AFTER DARK

The Albion ㉚ A barrage of sometimes humorous, sometimes
stark warning signs greet the unwary outside this traditional
Victorian street-corner pub. Inside the décor is packed with
ephemera from the early 20th century. Real ales are also a
speciality, as is simple and hearty food. Dedicated to 'grown-ups',
the Albion is serious about old-fashioned pub culture and is to
be avoided if you have children or are on tour with a stag
or hen group. ⓐ Park Street ① 01244 340345 ⓦ www.
albioninnchester.co.uk ⓛ 12.00–15.00 & 17.00–23.00 Mon–Sat,
12.00–14.30 & 19.00–22.30 Sun

Bar Lounge ㉛ Though just slightly out of the way from the rest
of Chester's drinking action, this large bar and restaurant is very
popular and guests are greeted by twinkling lights on the large
tree-fringed terrace. Dark and classy inside, chunky leather sofas

add to the relaxed and very friendly ambience, making it well liked by young professionals and fashionistas. **a** 75 Watergate Street **t** 01244 327394 **w** www.barlounge.co.uk **l** 11.00–24.00 Sun–Fri, 11.00–01.00 Sat

The Brewery Tap **32** Beer is king among the simple surroundings of this historic pub. Local brewery 'Spitting Feathers' is just one of the real ales that crowd its long bar, where locally sourced food is also championed. Charles I was

⏶ *Join one of the heritage open-top buses for a theatrical guided tour*

recorded as being courted here during his Civil War visit.
ⓐ 52–54 Lower Bridge Street ⓣ 01244 340999 ⓦ www.the-tap.
co.uk ⓛ 12.00–23.00 Mon–Sat, 12.00–22.30 Sun

Cruise ㉝ Take a voyage through six themed global destinations
of cool, spread over three extremely swish floors with each
theme more lavishly different and striking than the last. Live
music, themed parties and comedy nights also act as a magnet
to the glamorous of Chester. ⓐ 4 St John Street ⓣ 01244 408000
ⓦ www.cruisechester.com ⓛ 19.00–03.30 Mon & Thur, 19.00–
04.00 Fri & Sat, 19.00–02.00 Sun; closed Tues & Wed

D' Meltin' Pot ㉞ A relative newcomer, this is a lively
combination of bar, nightclub, live music and art venue along
with salsa and pole-dancing classes during the quieter week
nights and Sundays. Guest DJs help get partygoers to cut some
shapes with a broad spectrum of music genres. ⓐ 31 Watergate
Row ⓣ 01244 344651 ⓦ www.meltinpot.co.uk ⓛ 19.00–24.00
Tues & Wed, 19.00–02.00 Thur–Sat, 18.00–24.00 Sun;
closed Mon

The Pelican ㉟ This lovely spot attracts local media types, celebs
and the just plain fashionable. The inviting bar and interior lead
to a lovely walled garden at the rear that makes a perfect sun
trap during the late afternoon. Live music is provided on
Thursday evenings while upstairs hosts a highly regarded
brasserie. ⓐ 10 Commonhall Street ⓣ 01244 313258
ⓦ www.thechesterpelican.co.uk ⓛ 11.00–24.00 Mon–Wed,
11.00–01.00 Thur–Sat, 11.00–22.30 Sun

Outside the city centre

This rewarding area covers the attractions, sights, eating and drinking venues that surround the city walls and stretch into the city's suburbs. Some are within short, gentle walking distance of the city centre while others will require a car, bicycle or the help of public transport (see pages 37–8).

SIGHTS & ATTRACTIONS

Chester Boat
You can view the city, its surrounding meadows and wildlife from the River Dee on a 30-minute or two-hour cruise. Tickets can be purchased on board or from the **Chester Tourist Information Centre** (see page 93). Small discounts are available if combining a river cruise with the **Hop On Hop Off Bus Tours** (see pages 56–7). A commentary is given during the journey and a bar is available for light refreshments. Disco and BBQ cruises

HOLLYOAKS
Anyone poring over the maps, scratching their heads and wondering where the Chester suburb of Hollyoaks is will be disappointed. Devised by Phil Redmond and first aired in 1995, the eye-catching characters of this popular teen/young adult TV soap opera have been dealing with a whole baggage of dramatic themes in the fabled neighbourhood of the same name.

set sail every Saturday night for which reservations are required.
ⓐ The Groves ⓣ 01244 325394 ⓦ www.chesterboat.co.uk
ⓛ 11.00–17.00 every half hour daily (Easter–Oct); 11.00–16.00
every hour Sat & Sun, closed Mon–Fri (Nov–Mar)

Chester Boat Hire

If you fancy taking to the water of the River Dee under your own
steam, this company offers a choice of rowing, motor or pedal
boats. Prices start from £10 for 15 minutes of motorboat hire or
£10 for 45 minutes of rowing-boat action ⓐ The Groves
ⓣ 01244 400594 ⓦ www.chesterboathire.co.uk ⓛ 10.30–18.00
daily (summer only)

◭ Take a leisurely boat tour on the River Dee

Chester Racecourse

Even when quiet and out of season the 'Roodee' is quite a sight to behold and its turf can actually be trodden by visitors (entry is on Nun's Road) for free when there are no events taking place. It is not uncommon to see people taking their dogs for a walk around the circuit. Unusually for a racing circuit, the 1.65 km (1 mile and 49 yds) course is practically one long curve and it is actually possible to see all the racing action unfold without the aid of binoculars (see page 21).

Chester Zoo

Around 3.5 km (2 miles) from the city centre, this is a full day's outing in itself – 7,000 animals from 400 different species await inspection. There is a packed programme of daily events, posted

○ *A day at the zoo is fun for everyone*

RACECOURSE HISTORY

Chester racecourse sits on the site of a former river pool where once sat the giant Roman and medieval port of the city. There are remains of the Roman harbour wall still visible below Nun's Road. In the medieval period this part of the river silted up, creating an open meadow known as the 'Roodee' (after the Saxon word for 'cross' and the Norman word for 'island'). A form of football was played on the site until it was banned in 1533 for being too violent. Horse racing took over, the first recorded race being in 1539 with the consent of Chester's Lord Mayor, Henry Gee – whose surname gave rise to the term 'gee-gees'.

at the entrance, as well as exhibits detailing the work behind the scenes being done to protect endangered species and keep the collection alive and well. A monorail offers a great overview of the vast site, while a 15-minute boat ride gives an alternative perspective of some of the animal enclosures. Queuing for both may be necessary during the school holidays. The most popular animals are to the left of the park, so if arriving at a busy time, it may be worth heading anticlockwise towards the meerkats and rhinos and letting the crowds around the big blockbuster attractions thin out before you venture over there. ⓐ Upton-by-Chester ⓣ 01244 380280 ⓦ www.chesterzoo.org ⓛ 10.00–18.00 daily (spring & summer), 10.00–16.00 daily (autumn & winter); opening hours are adjusted to coincide with school holidays ⓝ Bus: 1. During the summer months, a shuttle bus operates from Chester railway station and is free to those in possession of a valid rail ticket. ❶ Admission charge (discounts available for those who arrive by bicycle); additional charges for monorail and boat ride

Grosvenor Park

This tranquil and colourful well-kept public space close to the city walls offers some fine views of the River Dee from the 'lookout' at its southern boundary. The 0.5-km (⅓-mile) track of the Grosvenor Park Miniature Railway around the park's central pond is a fun, albeit short, distraction for children. Among the tree-lined avenues, fragrant rockeries and lawn expanse, the

⬤ *Britain's largest remaining amphitheatre*

summer months see the arrival of outdoor theatre performances (see page 12). ⓐ Grosvenor Park Road ⓛ Dawn to dusk. Miniature railway ⓛ 10.30–17.00 daily (Apr–Oct), 11.00–16.00 Sun only (Nov–Mar) ⓘ Charge for railway

CULTURE

Chester Amphitheatre

Confirmed as the largest of its kind in Britain, this once-great Roman venue was first opened in the late 70s AD as a place for garrison training, public executions and recreational sports such as bull and bear baiting along with theatrical mock animal hunts. At its height, the arena could accommodate a braying crowd of up to 6,000, though today this once spectacular arena is barely a shadow of its former self. There is a series of information panels and a number of Roman recreation events take place during the summer months. ⓐ Pepper Street ⓦ www.english-heritage.org.uk ⓛ Daylight hours

Museum Gardens

Directly beneath city wall and once home to a flourishing clay-pipe industry (and a pit where cock fights were held) this narrow corridor now displays a crowded collection of the Roman architectural remains and ephemera unearthed in the city and repositioned here. There is plenty of information to hand on a collection of display boards. ⓐ The gardens can be entered from either The Groves or Little St John Street ⓛ Dawn to dusk ⓘ The entry on Little St John Street makes for an easier downhill route through the gardens.

RETAIL THERAPY

Immediately surrounding the city walls there is little to excite retail aficionados; however a short journey north unearths the vast Cheshire Oaks outlet centre (ⓐ Ellesmere Port ⓦ www.cheshireoaksdesigneroutlet.com ⓝ Bus: 1, 4, 4X), which offers all kinds of last season's designer and high-street wear collections at discounted prices.

TAKING A BREAK

Blue Moon Café £ ㊱ Its prime location on the riverbank, coupled with a startling 1950s–60s American diner interior, belies its country-cottage exterior. There is a seating area to the front and the main menu is dominated by all-day breakfasts, sandwiches, jacket potatoes and, in keeping with the 'Happy Days' ambience, ice-cream sundaes, though more substantial 'specials' are available. ⓐ The Groves ⓣ 01244 322481 ⓦ www.bluemooncafe.eu ⓛ 09.30–16.30 daily

The Café at the Walls £ ㊲ Not strictly speaking outside the city wall, rather attached to it, this no-nonsense café and takeaway offers a host of affordable light snacks, and substantial breakfast and lunch options including fish and chips. Go to the takeaway window overlooking the river and head to the waterside benches for a shared picnic with the ducks. ⓐ 13 Bridge Place ⓣ 01244 320275 ⓦ www.thecafeatthewalls.co.uk ⓛ 10.00–18.00 Tues–Sun, closed Mon

The Cheshire Cat £ 🔞 A 30-minute walk following the Shropshire Union Canal towpath south or a 15-minute journey by public transport, this large pub is a warm and cosy affair. It features a warren of traditional and tastefully decorated rooms and large outdoor spaces backing on to the picturesque canal. Cheerful staff serve up high-quality pub classics accompanied by choices from a specials board. 🄰 Whitchurch Road, Christleton 🅃 01244 332200 🅆 www.vintageinn.co.uk 🄻 12.00–22.00 Mon–Sat, 12.00–21.30 Sun 🄽 Bus: DB5, 41, 41A

Gate of India £ 🄴 In a city not renowned for Indian cuisine, this is a stand-out place for welcome and quality when only a traditional curry feast will do. Just 15 minutes from the eastern city wall, the samosas themselves are worth the walk. 🄰 25 City Road 🅃 01244 327 131 🄵 01244 349163 🄻 17.30–01.00 Mon–Thur, 17.30–02.00 Fri & Sat, 17.30–00.30 Sun

Hickory's £ 🄴 Hands-on food American style, this informal BBQ house makes little concession to non-carnivores but for the rest it does offer some fine smoked, sticky and occasionally fiery Tex-Mex cookin'. Located on the riverside, there is a large terrace to enjoy the water traffic views and wildlife during warmer months. 🄰 The Groves 🅃 01244 404000 🅆 www.hickorys.co.uk 🄻 11.00–23.00 daily

1539 £££ 🄴 A stylish and sassy open-plan restaurant within the racecourse complex, named after the year horse racing first began here. The inventive menu very much draws on new and classic British cuisine created with local ingredients (the herb garden is literally just outside) and all served with flair and conviviality. There is also plenty of open terrace space that during the daylight hours offers panoramic views of the ancient turf. Reservations recommended at weekends and a must during race meetings. ⓐ The Racecourse ⓣ 01244 304611 ⓦ www.restaurant1539.co.uk ⓛ 12.00–14.30 & 18.00–22.00 Mon–Thur, 12.00–15.30 & 18.00–22.00 Fri, 12.00–22.30 Sat, 12.00–19.00 Sun

AFTER DARK

The Chester Hangman ㊷ A 10-minute walk from the cathedral on a busy corner of the inner ring road is this small and fairly

⬤ *The Old Dee Bridge is the oldest bridge in the city*

low-key mock Tudor pub. However, for those who like their music loud and live, this is a good place to head for rock, folk and punk. Friendly bar staff and open mic and jam nights are hosted on Mondays and Thursdays. ⓐ 4–8 City Road ⓣ 01244 313965 ⓦ www.chesterhangman.co.uk ⓛ 12.00–01.00 Mon, 12.00–23.00 Tues & Wed, 12.00–late Thur–Sat, 12.00–23.00 Sun

Old Harkers Arms ⓭ The name suggests rural country pub; the reality is large converted canal-side warehouse space incorporating exposed brick walls and beams, topped off with a collection of decorative books and curios. Beer is taken seriously here, with regularly changing guest ales, and food is served until 21.30 every day. The prices are slightly higher than other places hereabouts but the conviviality and surroundings are worth the short walk beyond the city walls. ⓐ 1 Russell Street ⓣ 01244 344525 ⓦ www.harkersarms-chester.co.uk ⓛ 11.30–23.00 Mon–Sat, 12.00–22.30 Sun

The Ship Inn ⓮ A short walk across the River Dee into the quiet Handbridge suburb is worth the exercise if for no other reason than to get a drink or bite to eat and enjoy the grand views over the river from this smart hostelry. The bar is all dark woods and big sofas while the upstairs restaurant goes for bright and airy simplicity with a menu focusing on classic British and Tex-Mex food sourced from local suppliers. Extremely child friendly, live jazz and soul along with quiz nights raise the volume level come nightfall. ⓐ 18 Handbridge ⓣ 01244 678400 ⓦ www. theshipchester.com ⓛ 09.00–23.00 Mon–Sat, 10.00–22.00 Sun ⓝ Bus: DB1, DB2, DB5

Telford's Warehouse ⓯ Named after the 18th-century boy wonder engineer Thomas Telford, this former canal building has been sympathetically converted to provide an interesting place to both eat and drink. More than anything else though, this is one of the places in the city to catch rising and established live musical talent and comes with a long and very illustrious lineage of previous musical performances. Real-ale drinkers should be kept content too and it also boasts a pleasant waterside open terrace, all just a short walk from the cathedral. ⓐ Tower Wharf, Raymond Street ⓣ 01244 390090 ⓦ www.telfordswarehousechester.com ⓛ 12.00–23.00 Mon & Tues, 12.00–01.00 Wed, 12.00–00.30 Thur, 12.00–02.00 Fri & Sat, 12.00–01.00 Sun

NOWHERE

In the nearby suburb of Handbridge, just across the River Dee on a track between the Old Dee Bridge and Edgar Fields Park, is the intriguingly named 18th-century 'Nowhere' cottage. There are a number of theories as to how it came by this name, but there is strong speculation that it inspired John Lennon to write 'Nowhere Man' after hearing of its existence during a 1963 Beatles' gig in the city.

● *Beautiful Tatton Park estate*

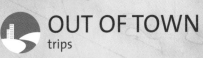 OUT OF TOWN
trips

Llandudno

Llandudno is a study in elegance, quietly basking in a renaissance of seaside fashionability. A sweeping promenade separates handsome townhouse hotels, chic guest houses and traditional B&Bs from the beach. Flamboyant flowers, the historic pier, donkey rides and regular outdoor entertainment add a taste of old-fashioned fun, all overlooked by the towering headland of history and myth, the Great Orme. For further questions and queries on the area, the friendly staff at **Llandudno Tourist Information Centre** should have the solution. ⓐ Library Building, Mostyn Street ⓣ 01492 577577 ⓦ www.visitllandudno.org.uk ⓛ 09.00–17.00 Mon–Sat, closed Sun

GETTING THERE

The 76-km (47-mile) journey by car should take no longer than an hour to complete following the A55. The train provides an excellent alternative option (Arriva Trains ⓣ 0845 606 1660 ⓦ www.arrivatrainswales.co.uk), taking just over an hour.

SIGHTS & ATTRACTIONS

Boat Trips

The Llandudno Boat Company offers short speedboat rides around the bay (ⓣ (01492) 878228 ⓦ www.llandudnoboattrips. co.uk ⓛ Apr–Sept), while the **Great Gussie** and **Neptune** provide more gentle sailings (ⓣ 07961 561589 ⓛ Daily Easter–Oct).

Bus Tour

A one-hour double-decker tour takes in Llandudno and neighbouring Conwy. Ticket holders can alight and rejoin at any stop over a 24-hour period. ⓐ North Parade (opposite Llandudno Pier) ⓣ 01492 879133 ⓦ www.city-sightseeing.com ⓛ Mar–Oct ⓘ Admission charge

Great Orme

This dominant headland offers an array of things to do and see. Try the Cable Car (ⓐ Happy Valley Gardens ⓣ 01492 877205 ⓦ www.llandudnoattractions.com ⓛ 10.00–17.00 daily ⓘ Admission charge); alternatively, a Victorian Tram makes the ascent every 20 minutes (ⓐ Church Walks ⓣ 01492 879306 ⓦ www.greatormetramway.co.uk ⓛ 10.00–18.00 daily (Apr–Sept); 10.00–17.00 daily (Mar & Oct)). The most rewarding

⬥ The promenade at Llandudno

aspect of the summit is the vista over the bay and North Wales. A car park and a visitors' centre are also here.

Great Orme Mines

Here is a great chance to explore a network of tunnels created during the Bronze Age. Back above ground, nature lovers will enjoy the wild flowers, sea bird colonies and ruminating sheep. ❶ 01492 870447 Ⓦ www.greatormemines.info ❸ 10.00–16.30 daily (late Mar–Oct) ❶ Admission charge Ⓝ Tram

Llandudno Pier

One of the best-preserved piers of its kind in the UK, a stroll along its almost 700-m (2,295-ft) extent is a journey among candy floss, saucy postcards, CDs and cheap mementoes. There are a number of amusements and places for a drink plus great views of the bay at the pier end. ❸ 10.00–18.00 daily

St Tudno's Church

Perched astride the Great Orme, this ancient church is used to great effect during the summer when it hosts outdoor services. Ⓦ www.llandudno-parish.org.uk/index.html ❸ Daily (Apr–Oct); open Sat, Sun, Wed & bank hols (Nov–Mar)

CULTURE

Llandudno Museum

The town's long history is brought together in this small collection of artefacts and tableaux. ❹ 17 Golddaeth Street ❶ 01492 876517 ❺ llandudno.museum@lineone.net

🕐 10.30–13.00 & 14.00–17.00 Tues–Sat, 14.15–17.00 Sun (summer); 13.30–16.30 Tues–Sat (winter), closed Sun & Mon

Oriel Mostyn Gallery

Llandudno's foremost collection of local and international contemporary art. 🅰 12 Vaughan Street 🕿 01492 879201 🌐 www.mostyn.org 🕐 10.00–17.00 Mon–Sat, closed Sun

RETAIL THERAPY

The most rewarding shopping area is on the upper stretches of **Mostyn Street**, at Clare's department store (🅰 97–99 Mostyn Street 🕿 01492 876711) or the small Victoria Shopping Centre (🅰 48 Mostyn Street 🌐 www.victoriacentre.net).

TAKING A BREAK

Badgers Tea Rooms £ This old-school example of hospitality and ambience serves a selection of light savoury bites and substantial cakes. 🅰 The Victoria Centre, 48 Mostyn Street 🕿 01492 871649 🌐 www.badgerstearooms.co.uk 🕐 09.30–17.00 Mon–Sat; 11.00–16.00 Sun (Mar–Dec)

AFTER DARK

Terrace Restaurant ££ Experience excellently cooked local foods at this award-winning restaurant overlooking the bay. 🅰 St George's Hotel, The Promenade 🕿 01492 877544 🌐 www.stgeorgeswales.co.uk 🕐 18.00–20.45 daily

Vale Royal, Cheshire

East of Chester, the pastoral verdancy of the landscapes, picturesque well-to-do villages and a collection of unique attractions certainly make this often overlooked part of Britain worthy of some exploration.

GETTING THERE

There are regular hourly rail services taking just over 30 minutes (see page 90) and an hourly bus (service number 82) that takes under an hour (see pages 37–8). Drivers will find the A51, A54 and A556 whisking them to the town of Northwich at the heart of this area in under 40 minutes.

SIGHTS & ATTRACTIONS

Anderton Boat Lift

One of the wonders of the canal network, this giant boat lift comes with a visitors' centre, café and cruises that take visitors

VALE ROYAL

Vale Royal is said to derive from the 13th century. Returning from the Crusades Prince Edward (latterly Edward I) was so relieved at surviving a violent sea storm that in thanks he founded an abbey in what he described as 'Vale Royal, the fairest vale in all England'.

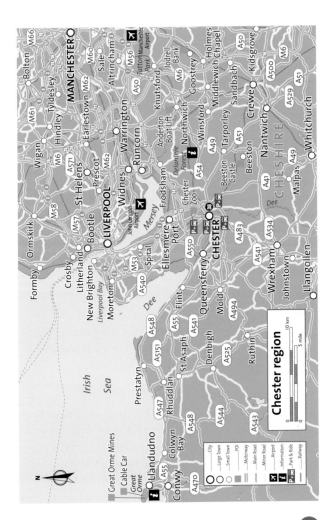

through this monumental shipping elevator. ⓐ Lift Lane,
Northwich ⓣ 01606 786777 ⓦ www.andertonboatlift.co.uk
ⓛ 10.00–17.00 daily (Mar–start of Oct); 11.00–16.00 Wed–Sun,
closed Mon & Tues (Oct); contact in advance for winter cruise
times ⓘ Admission charge ⓝ Bus: 82 & 4 (approx 1½ hours with
15-minute walk)

Beeston Castle

Perched atop a sheer rocky crag, Beeston offers 4,000 years of
history and some of the best views from fortifications in
England. ⓐ Chapel Lane, Beeston, Tarporley ⓣ 01829 260464
ⓦ www.english-heritage.org.uk/beeston ⓛ 10.00–18.00 daily
(Apr–Sept); 10.00–16.00 Thur–Mon, closed Tues & Wed (Oct–
Mar) ⓘ Admission and car park charge. Unavoidable steep walk
to the castle ⓝ Bus: 84 & 56 (approx 2 hours and walk)

⬤ Dare to ascend the steep steps to Beeston Castle

Delamere Forest

This shady woodland is a haven for nature lovers, walkers, cyclists and for those who like a little tree-top adventure (ⓐ Delamere Visitor Centre, Northwich ⓣ 01606 889792 ⓛ 10.00–17.00 daily (summer), 10.00–16.00 daily (winter)). Start at **Linmere Lodge**, where there is a fee-paying car park, information centre, shop, café and cycle hire place (ⓐ Linmere Lodge ⓣ 07949 088477 ⓦ www.tracs-uk.co.uk ⓛ 10.00–18.00 daily). **Go Ape** offers swings, rope bridges and zip wires for high-flying tree canopy exhilaration. ⓐ Linmere Lodge ⓣ 0845 643 9215 ⓦ www.goape.co.uk ⓛ Call in advance ⓘ Restrictions apply. Admission fee ⓝ Train: Delamere

Jodrell Bank

Home to the world-famous Lovell telescope and Radio Astronomy Observatory, star gazing, exhibitions and a Galaxy Maze will inspire scientists young and old. ⓐ Holmes Chapel ⓣ 01477 571339 ⓦ www.manchester.ac.uk/jodrellbank/viscen ⓛ 10.30–17.00 daily (Apr–Oct); 10.30–15.00 Tues–Fri, 11.00–16.00 Sat & Sun, closed Mon (Nov–Mar) ⓘ Admission charge ⓝ Train: Goostrey then 4 km (2½ miles) walk

Tatton Park

One of the country's most impressive estates offers a deer park, award-winning gardens, a grand mansion house and rare breed farm. This is also home to the hugely popular Royal Horticultural Society's Show held each July. ⓐ Knutsford ⓣ 01625 374400 ⓦ www.tattonpark.org.uk ⓛ Tues–Sun 10.00–17.00, closed Mon (summer); Tues–Sun 11.00–15.00, closed Mon (winter) ⓘ Admission charge

RETAIL THERAPY

The centres of **Tarporley** and **Knutsford** are a nice diversion for their upmarket high-street family-run businesses. The vast and bargain-filled Bookstore is worth a visit. ⓐ Chester Road, Oakmere nr Northwich ⓣ 01606 883750 ⓛ 09.30–17.30 Mon–Sat, 11.00–17.00 Sun

TAKING A BREAK

Vale Royal Abbey Arms £ The imposing sandstone exterior reveals a tastefully decorated collection of nooks and crannies.
ⓐ Chester Road, Oakmere ⓣ 01606 882747
ⓦ www.vale-royal-abbey-arms-northwich.co.uk
ⓛ 12.00–22.00 daily

AFTER DARK

Stuart's Table at the Farmers Arms ££ This award-winning restaurant serves British seasonal food. ⓐ Huxley Lane, Huxley
ⓣ 01829 781342 ⓦ www.stuartstable.co.uk ⓛ (dining) 17.30–20.30 Mon, 12.00–14.00 & 17.30–21.00 Tues–Sat, 12.00–17.00 Sun

Cabbage Hall £££ The British cuisine here is sourced seasonally and from the local landscape. ⓐ Forest Road, Little Budworth
ⓣ 01829 760292 ⓦ www.cabbagehallrestaurant.com
ⓛ 12.00–21.00 Mon–Fri, 12.00–22.00 Sat, 12.00–19.00 Sun

● *Spend a peaceful day at Tatton Park*

PRACTICAL
information

Directory

GETTING THERE
By air

Liverpool John Lennon Airport (☎ 0871 521 8484 ⓦ www.liverpoolairport.com) is approximately 45 minutes by car or 1½ hours by train (via Lime Street Station) and is served by international and national budget airline services such as **easyJet** (ⓦ www.easyjet.com) and **Ryanair** (ⓦ www.ryanair.com). The nearest major international airport is **Manchester** (☎ 08712 710711 ⓦ www.manchesterairport.co.uk) with a journey time of 50 minutes by car or 1 hour 10 minutes by train via Manchester's Piccadilly Station.

By rail

Chester is well served with direct access to major UK cities including regular services on the West Coast Main Line to London, a journey of just over two hours. **National Rail** ☎ 0845 748 4950 ⓦ www.nationalrail.co.uk

By road

The M56, which is fed by the M6 and subsequently all points north and south in the UK, is the major motorway that comes closest to Chester. Spokes of leafy suburban roads offer a number of ways in to Chester, though at peak times these can be busy. To avoid traffic congestion and sometimes hefty central parking fees, look into the four **Park & Ride** car parks surrounding the city that offer frequent bus transfers in and out of the city centre. ⓦ www.cheshirewestandchester.gov.uk/transport.

National Express Coaches have regular services from across the UK, including up to three services a day from London's Victoria Coach Station. 🕿 0871 781 8178 🅦 www.nationalexpress.com

By ferry

Chester is only a two-hour road or rail journey from the port of Holyhead, using **Stena Line** to make the Irish Sea crossing, (🅦 www.stenaline.co.uk 🕿 08447 707 070) or one hour from the port of Liverpool aboard **P&O Ferries** (🕿 0871 664 5645 🅦 www.poferries.com). Visitors from Northern Ireland can travel via Liverpool and should contact **Norfolk Line** (🕿 0844 847 5042 🅦 www.norfolkline.com).

HEALTH, SAFETY AND CRIME

Chester has no reputation for serious crime, but precautions should always be employed to keep money, cameras and phones tucked away. When using ATMs it's wise to shield the screen and keyboard. In terms of health, Chester's tap water is fine to drink.

EMERGENCY CONTACTS
Police

If there is a crime in progress or danger to life requiring police, fire or ambulance 🕿 999. For non-emergencies call the Cheshire Constabulary 🕿 0845 458 0000 🅦 www.cheshire.police.uk

Medical services

Late-night pharmacy: Co-op Pharmacy ⓐ 12 Upper Northgate Street 🕿 01904 656360 🕘 09.00–21.00 Mon–Sat, 10.00–21.00 Sun

The Countess of Chester Hospital in the northern suburbs of the city includes both accident and emergency services as well as a walk-in centre for minor injuries and illnesses.

ⓐ Liverpool Road ⓣ 01244 365000 ⓦ www.coch.nhs.uk
Ⓝ Bus: 1, 2, 3, CTT3

For medical advice contact NHS Direct for 24-hour telephone information. ⓣ 0845 4647 ⓦ www.nhsdirect.nhs.uk

For emergency dental issues during normal working hours call the local NHS helpline (ⓣ 01244 650368) for advice. For out of hours advice (ⓛ 18.00–22.00 Mon–Fri) ⓣ 07748 654782. On weekends and bank holidays contact the emergency clinics.
ⓣ 01244 356802 ⓛ 10.00–12.00 & 14.00–16.00

OPENING HOURS

Most of Chester's shops are open from between 09.00 and 10.00 through to 17.30, Monday to Saturday, and from 11.00 until 16.00 on Sunday. Some smaller convenience stores outside the city walls trade from earlier till later. Almost all shops and attractions are open on bank holidays except Christmas Day and Easter Sunday. Banks in the city are open between 09.30 and 16.30 Monday to Friday; many also open on Saturday mornings. ATMs are widely available for cash withdrawals.

TOILETS

The following companies have agreed to let the public use their conveniences without buying anything! Burger King (ⓐ Foregate Street), Tesco (ⓐ Frodsham Street), Little Roodee Café (ⓐ Little Roodee Car Park) and the Slug & Lettuce

(ⓐ Bridge Street). There are also well-maintained facilities at the Pepper Street entrance to the Grosvenor Shopping Centre.

CHILDREN
Some of the attractions such as the Grosvenor Museum and Dewa Roman Experience (see page 58) go to some lengths to get the young ones engaged with their historical exhibits. Feed the birds at the Groves alongside the River Dee or head to the nearby Grosvenor Park for a short miniature railway ride during the summer. A little way out of the city is Chester Zoo (see pages 70–72) and, in the opposite direction, the seaside fun of Llandudno.

TRAVELLERS WITH DISABILITIES
To enjoy the freedom of the city, visitors can use the Shopmobility scheme, which offers rental services on equipment including wheelchairs and scooters. ⓐ Frodsham Street Car Park, Frodsham Street ☎ 01244 312626 🕐 10.00–16.00 daily

FURTHER INFORMATION
Chester Tourist Information Centre
ⓐ Town Hall, Northgate Street ☎ 0845 647 7868
ⓦ www.visitchester.com
ⓔ welcome@visitchesterandcheshire.co.uk 🕐 09.00–17.30 Mon–Sat; 10.00–17.00 Sun & bank holiday Mon (closed Christmas Day, Boxing Day and New Year's Day)
ⓦ www.visitcheshire.com
ⓦ www.chesterwalls.info
ⓦ www.chesternights.com